AUDIO ACCESS INCLUDED
Recorded Piano Accompaniments Online

PLAYBACK+
Speed • Pitch • Balance • Loop

SINGER'S JAZZ ANTHOLOGY | LOW VOICE

christmas standards

Arranged by Brent Edstrom

T0079501

To access audio visit:
www.halleonard.com/mylibrary

"Enter Code"
2400-9361-6502-7563

ISBN 978-1-5400-9519-0

HAL•LEONARD®

Visit Hal Leonard Online at
www.halleonard.com

Contact us:
Hal Leonard
7777 West Bluemound Road
Milwaukee, WI 53213
Email: info@halleonard.com

In Europe, contact:
Hal Leonard Europe Limited
42 Wigmore Street
Marylebone, London, W1U 2RN
Email: info@halleonardeurope.com

In Australia, contact:
Hal Leonard Australia Pty. Ltd.
4 Lentara Court
Cheltenham, Victoria, 3192 Australia
Email: info@halleonard.com.au

ARRANGER'S NOTE

The vocalist's part in the *Singer's Jazz Anthology* matches the original sheet music but is *not* intended to be sung verbatim. Instead, melodic embellishments and alterations of rhythm and phrasing should be incorporated to both personalize a performance and conform to the accompaniments. In some cases, the form has been expanded to include "tags" and other endings not found in the original sheet music. In these instances, the term *ad lib.* indicates new melodic material appended to the original form.

Although the concept of personalizing rhythms and embellishing melodies might seem awkward to singers who specialize in classical music, there is a long tradition of melodic variation within the context of performance dating back to the Baroque. Not only do jazz singers personalize a given melody to fit the style of an accompaniment, they also develop a distinctive sound that helps *further* personalize their performances. Undoubtedly, the best strategy for learning how to stylize a jazz melody is to listen to recordings from the vocal jazz canon, including artists such as Nat King Cole, Ella Fitzgerald, Billie Holiday, Frank Sinatra, Sarah Vaughan, Nancy Wilson, and others.

The accompaniments in the *Singer's Jazz Anthology* can also be embellished by personalizing rhythms or dynamics, and chord labels are provided for pianists who are comfortable playing their own chord voicings. In some cases, optional, written-out improvisations are provided. These can be performed "as is," embellished, or skipped, depending on the performers' preference.

The included audio features piano recordings that can be used as a rehearsal aid or to accompany a performance. Tempi were selected to fit the character of each accompaniment, and the optional piano solos were omitted to provide a more seamless singing experience for vocalists who utilize them as backing tracks.

I hope you find many hours of enjoyment exploring the *Singer's Jazz Anthology* series!

Brent Edstrom

ALL I WANT FOR CHRISTMAS IS YOU

Words and Music by MARIAH CAREY
and WALTER AFANASIEFF

I don't want a lot ____ for Christ-mas, there is just one thing ____
I won't ask for much ____ this Christ-mas, I won't e-ven wish ____

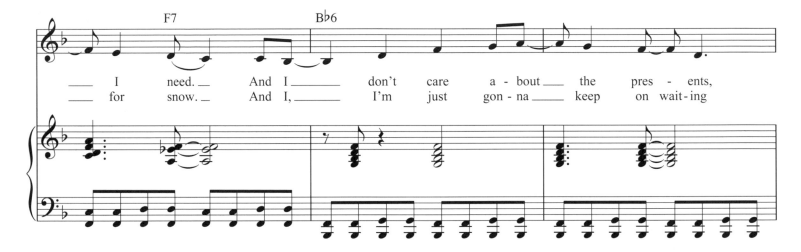

____ I need. ____ And I ____ don't care a-bout ____ the pres-ents,
____ for snow. ____ And I, ____ I'm just gon-na ____ keep on wait-ing

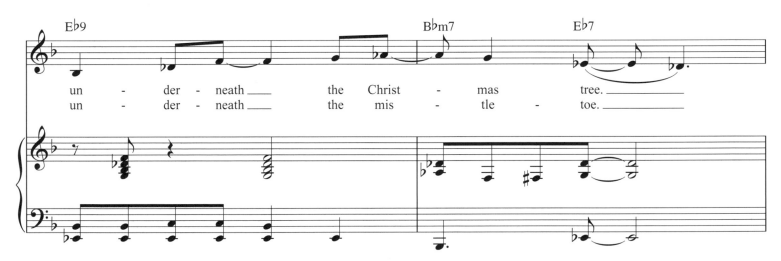

un - der - neath ____ the Christ - mas tree. ____
un - der - neath ____ the mis - tle - toe. ____

I don't need ____ to hang ____ my stock-ing there up-on ____ the fi -
I won't make ____ a list ____ and send ____ it to the North ____ Pole for
I don't want ____ a lot ____ for Christ - mas, this is all ____ I'm ask -

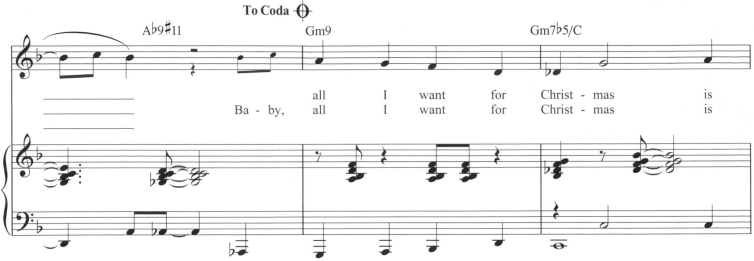

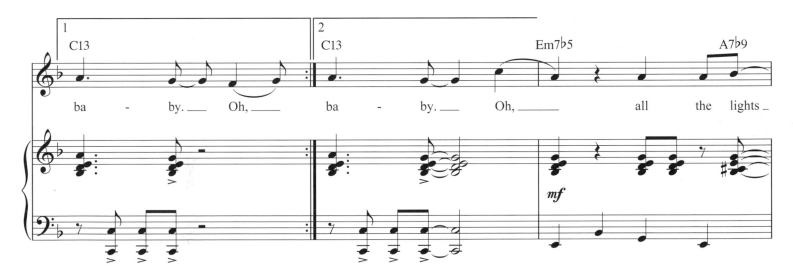

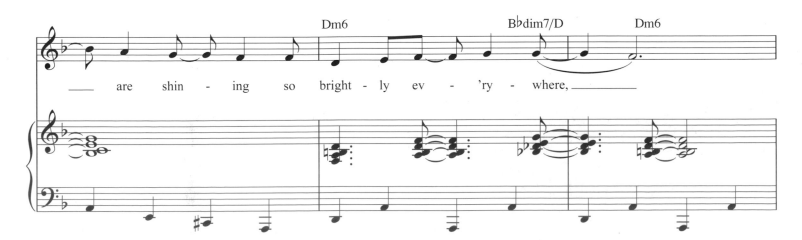

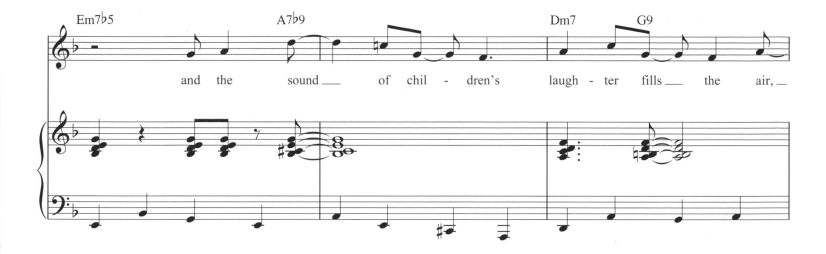

and the sound ___ of chil-dren's laugh-ter fills ___ the air, ___

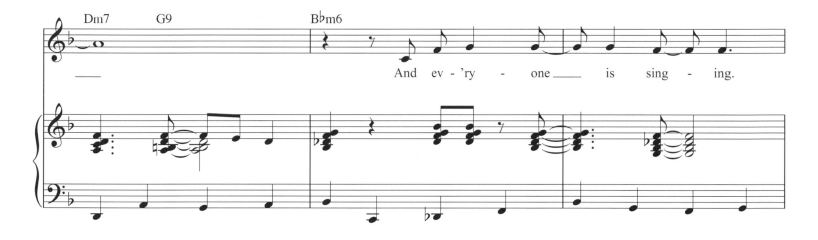

___ And ev-'ry - one ___ is sing - ing.

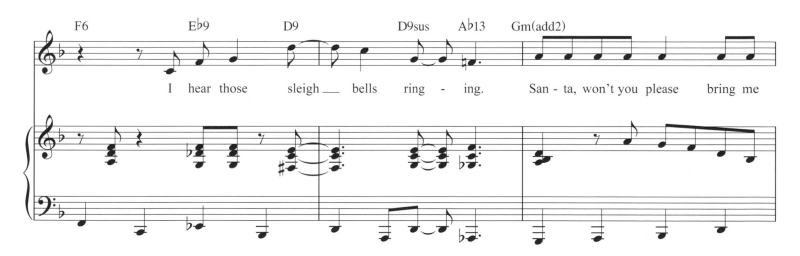

I hear those sleigh ___ bells ring - ing. San - ta, won't you please bring me

D.S. al Coda

what I real - ly need, won't you please bring my ba - by to me. ___ Oh, ___

CODA

all I want for Christ-mas _____ is _____

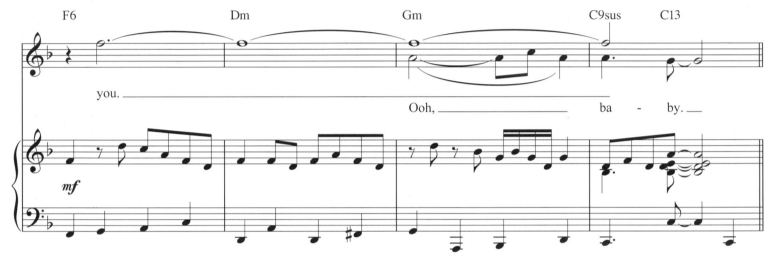

you. _____
Ooh, _____ ba - by. ___

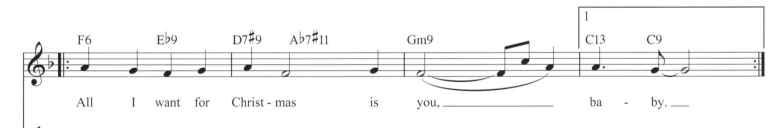

All I want for Christ-mas is you, _____ ba - by. ___

ba - by. ___ you.

BLUE CHRISTMAS

Words and Music by BILLY HAYES
and JAY JOHNSON

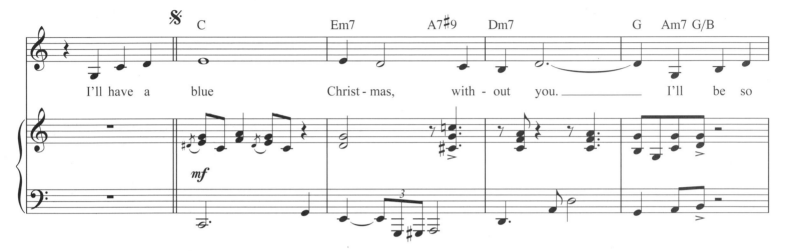

I'll have a blue Christ-mas, with-out you. _____ I'll be so

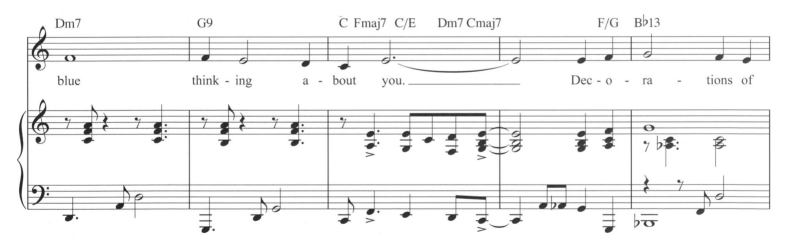

blue think-ing a-bout you. _____ Dec-o-ra-tions of

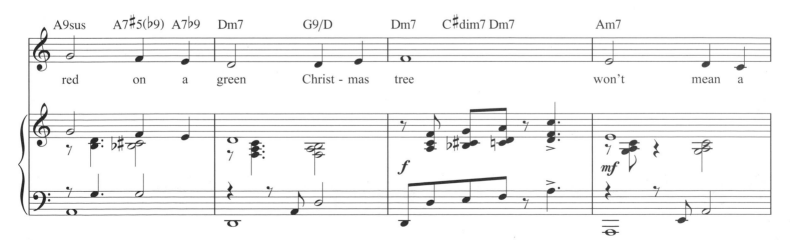

red on a green Christ-mas tree won't mean a

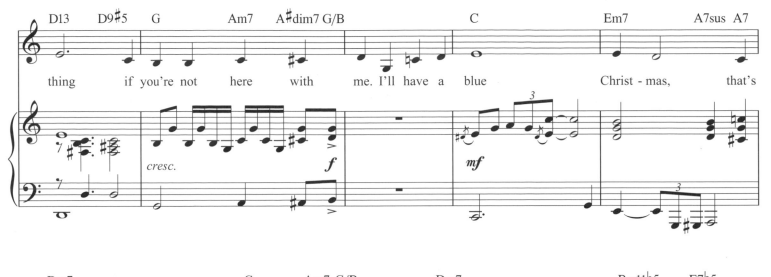

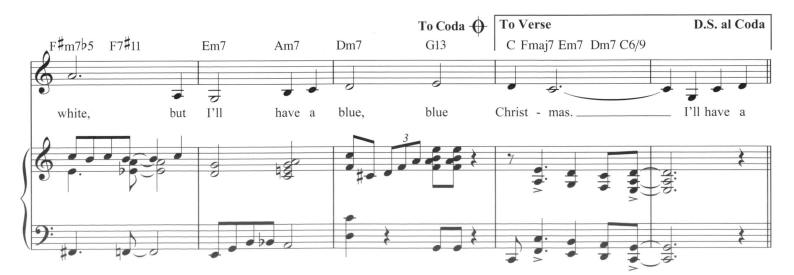

To Opt. Piano Solo

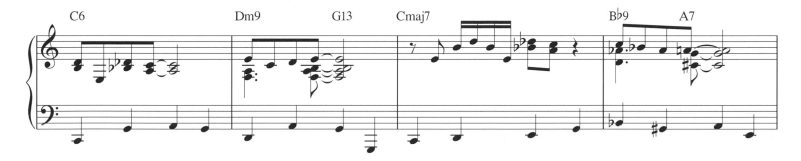

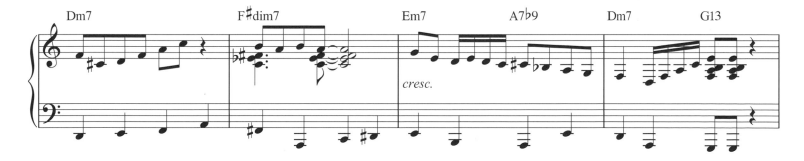

D.S. al Coda

CODA **Straight 8ths**

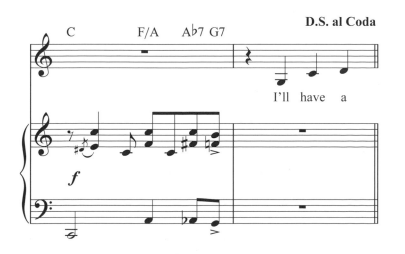

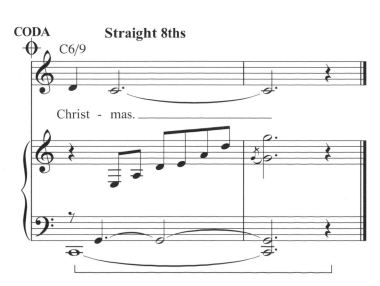

THE CHRISTMAS SONG
(Chestnuts Roasting on an Open Fire)

Music and Lyric by MEL TORMÉ
and ROBERT WELLS

CHRISTMAS TIME IS HERE
from A CHARLIE BROWN CHRISTMAS

Words by LEE MENDELSON
Music by VINCE GUARALDI

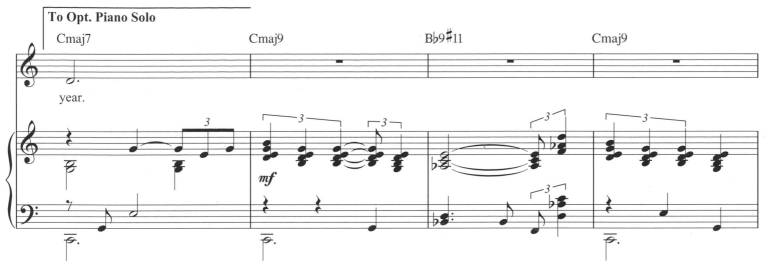

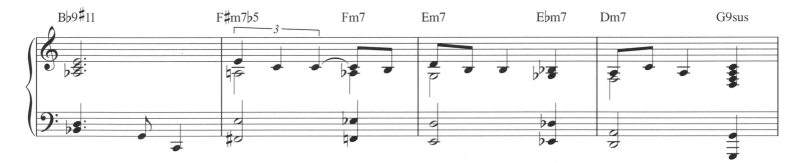

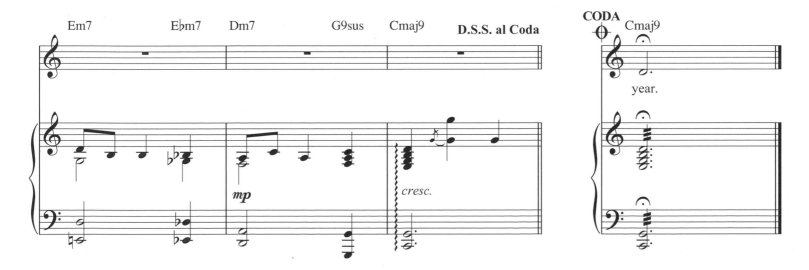

FROSTY THE SNOW MAN

Words and Music by STEVE NELSON
and JACK ROLLINS

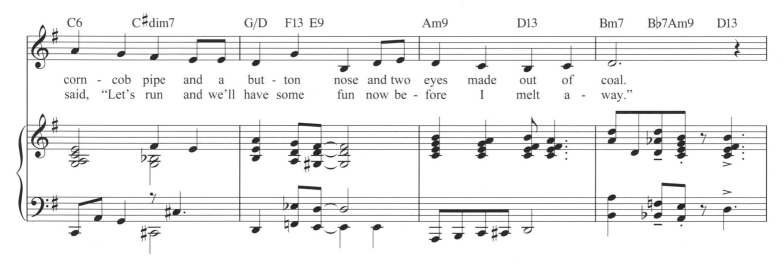

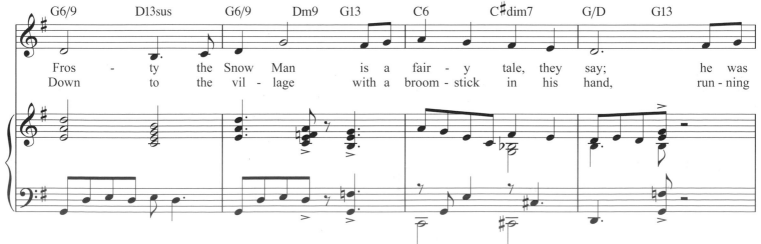

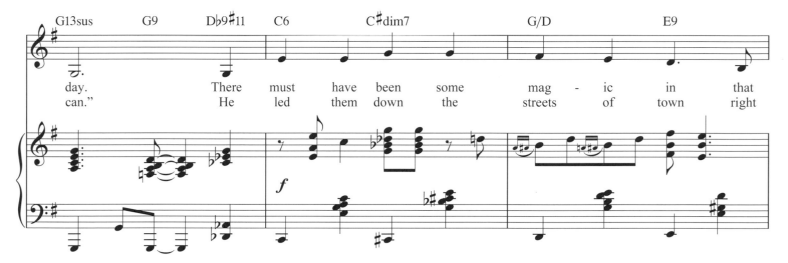

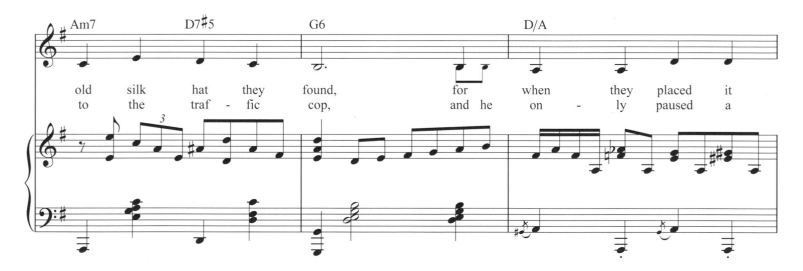

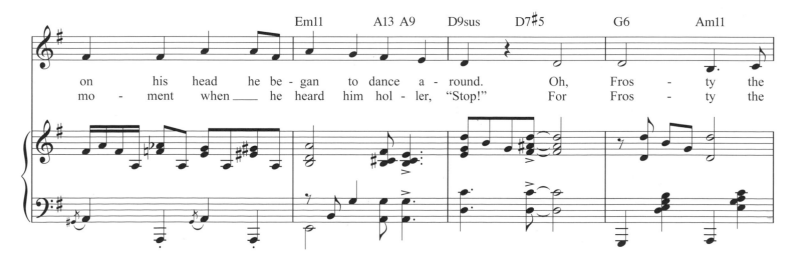

G6/B Dm9 G13 C6 C♯dim7 G6/D G6 C6 C♯dim7
Snow Man was a - live as he could be, and the chil - dren say he could
Snow Man had to hur - ry on his way, but he waved good-bye say - in',
G6 F7♯11 E7 Am7 D7 G C7 G/D
laugh and play just the same as you and me.
"Don't you cry, I'll be back a - gain some - day."
G6/9 B♭/D Gmaj7 B♭/D G6/9 Am7 D9
Thump-et - y thump thump, thump-et - y thump thump, look at Fros - ty go.
mp lightly
mf
D13sus Gm7/D D9sus E♭m(maj7)/D Am9 D13 Am7/D A♯dim7/D G6/D
Thump-et - y thump thump, thump-et - y thump thump, o-ver the hills of snow.
mp
cresc.
ff
mp
8vb

(There's No Place Like)
HOME FOR THE HOLIDAYS

Words and Music by AL STILLMAN
and ROBERT ALLEN

Moderate Swing

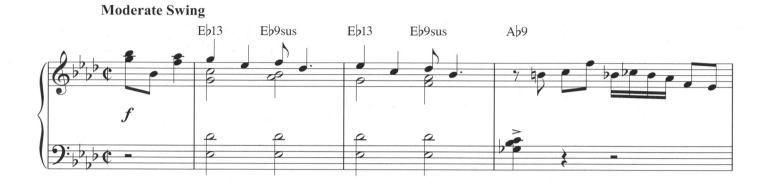

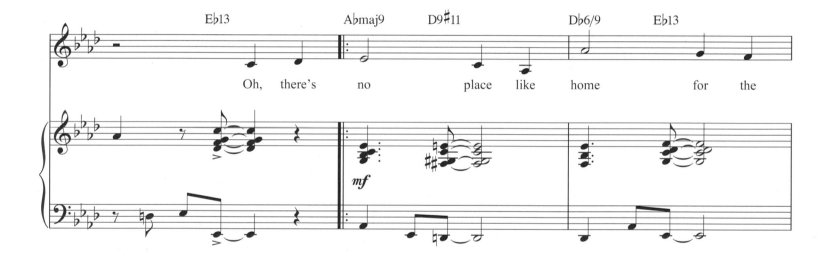

Oh, there's no place like home for the

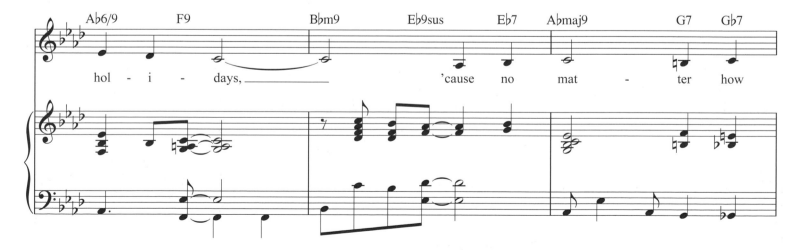

hol-i-days, _____ 'cause no mat-ter how

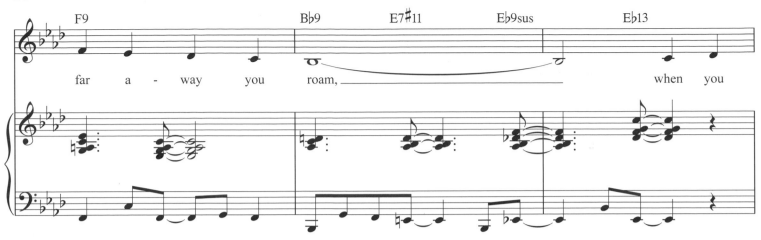

far a - way you roam, _____ when you

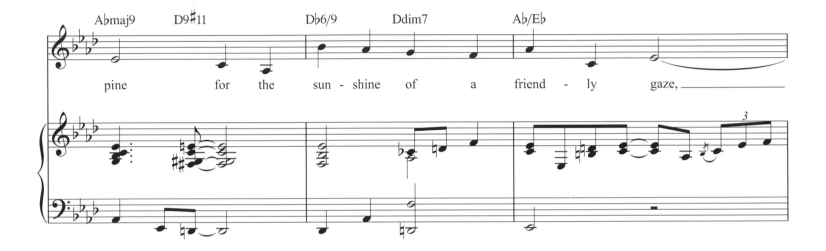

pine for the sun - shine of a friend - ly gaze, _____

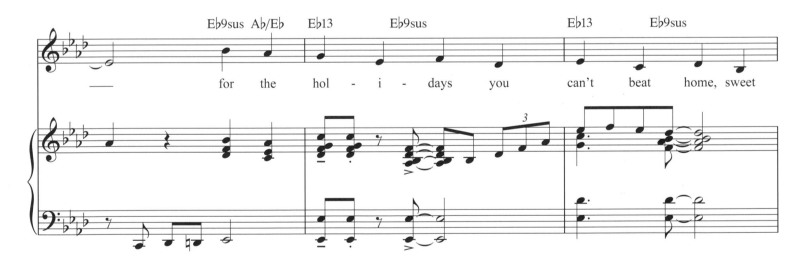

_____ for the hol - i - days you can't beat home, sweet

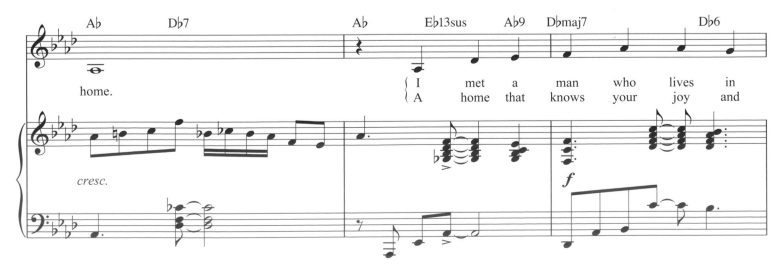

home.

I met a man who lives in
A home that knows your joy and

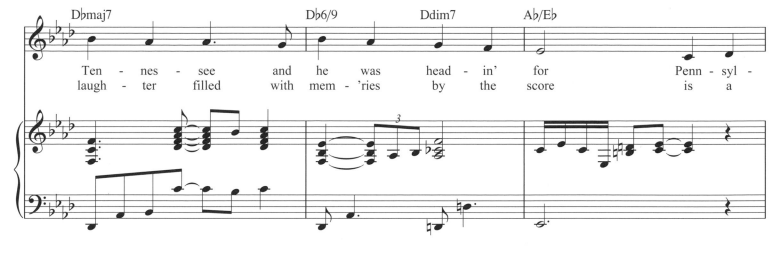

Tennessee and he was headin' for Pennsyl-
laughter filled with mem'ries by the score is a

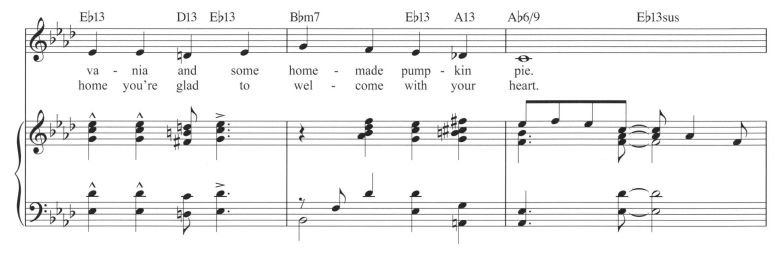

-vania and some home-made pumpkin pie.
home you're glad to welcome with your heart.

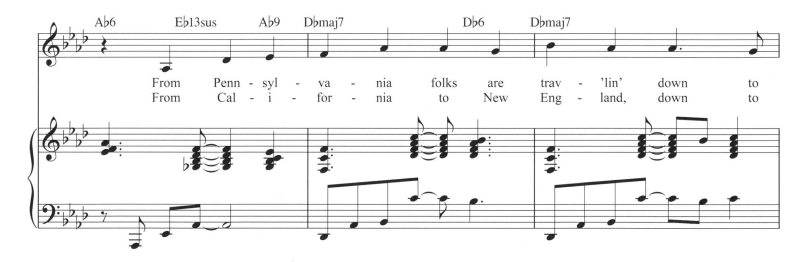

From Pennsylvania folks are trav'lin' down to
From California to New England, down to

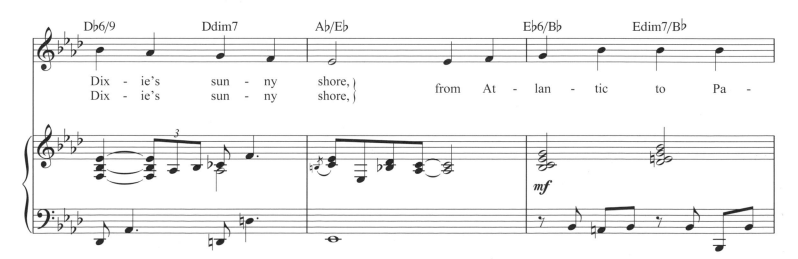

Dixie's sunny shore,
Dixie's sunny shore, from Atlantic to Pa-

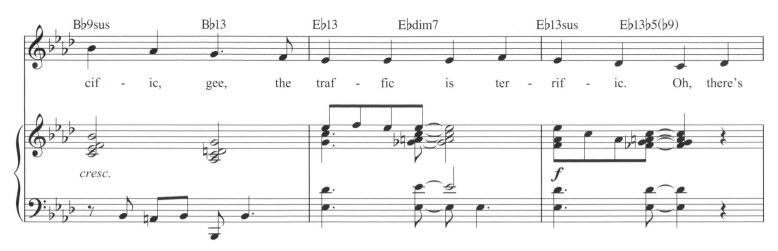

cif - ic, gee, the traf - fic is ter - rif - ic. Oh, there's

no place like home for the hol - i - days, ____

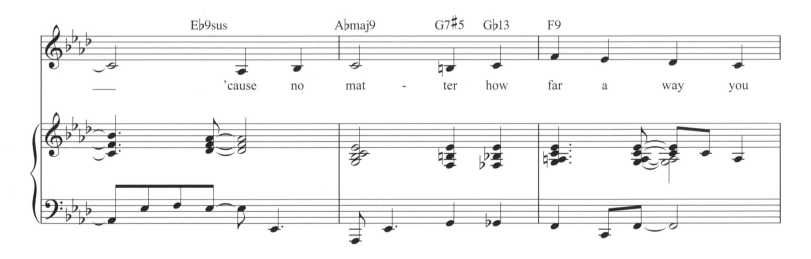

____ 'cause no mat - ter how far a way you

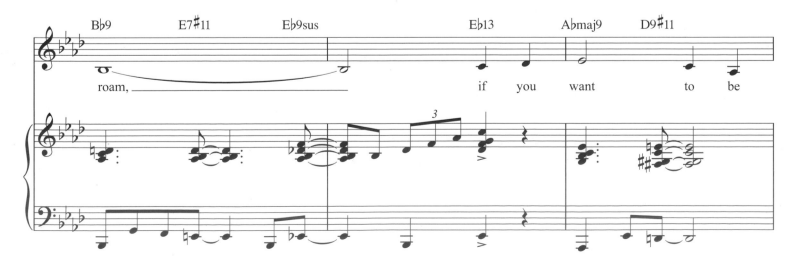

roam, ____ if you want to be

HAVE YOURSELF A MERRY LITTLE CHRISTMAS

from MEET ME IN ST. LOUIS

Words and Music by HUGH MARTIN
and RALPH BLANE

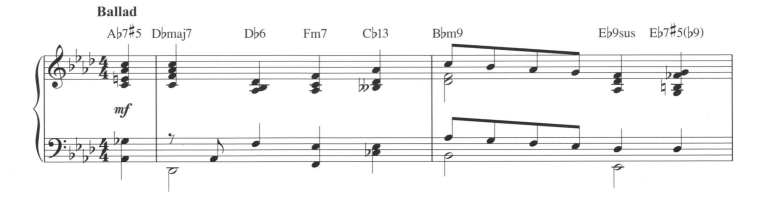

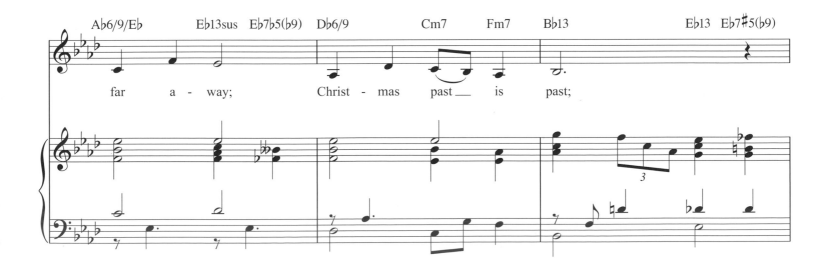

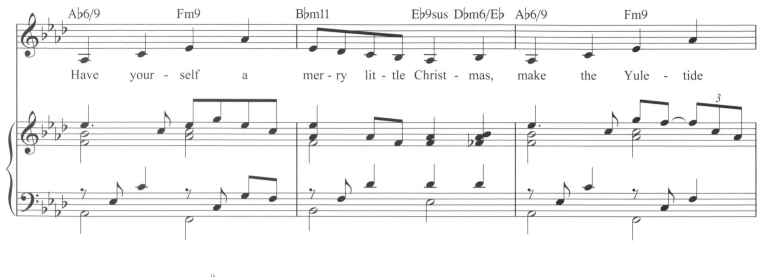

Lilting Swing

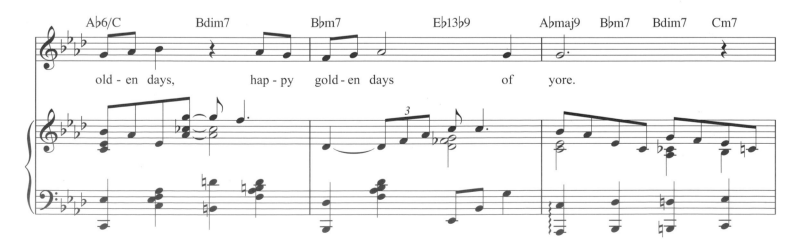

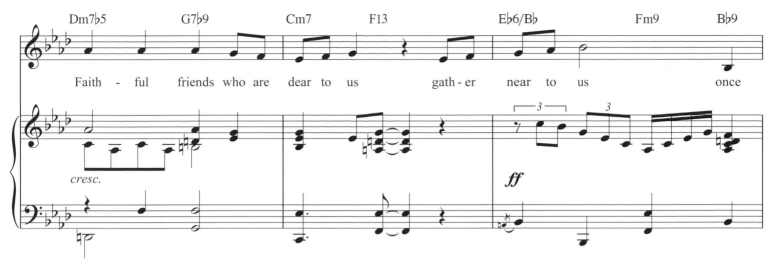

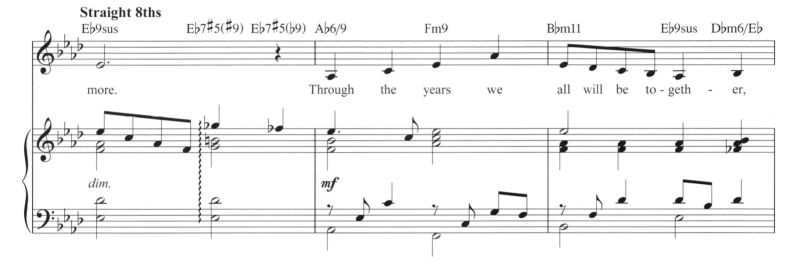

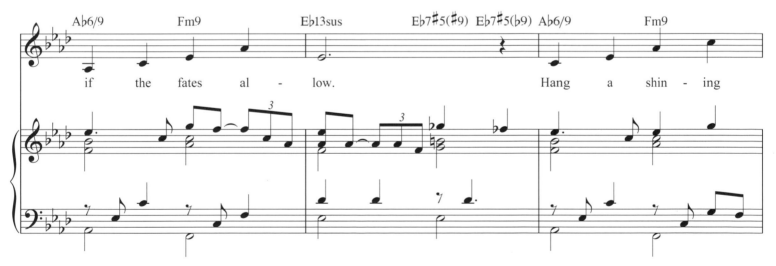

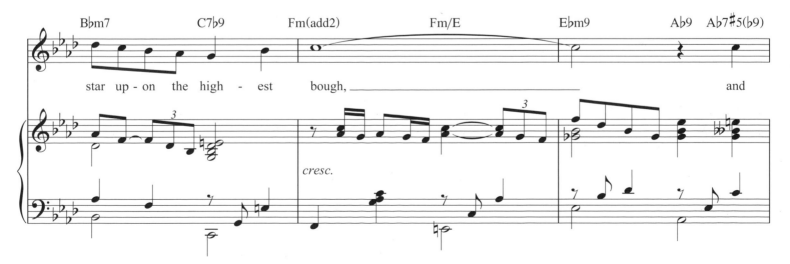

Dbmaj7 Db6 Bbm9 Eb9sus Eb7b9 Ab6/9 Fm9 Em9

have your-self a mer-ry lit-tle Christ-mas now.

Swing 8ths

Ebm9 D9#11 Dbmaj13 Dbm(maj13) Ab6/C Bdim7

Here we are as in old-en days, hap-py

Bbm7 Eb13b9 Abmaj9 Bbm7 Bdim7 Cm7 Dm7b5 G7b9

gold-en days of yore. Faith-ful friends who are

Straight 8ths

Cm7 F13 Eb/Bb Fm9 Bb13 Eb9sus Eb13

dear to us gath-er near to us once more.

I HEARD THE BELLS
ON CHRISTMAS DAY

Words by HENRY WADSWORTH LONGFELLOW
Adapted by JOHNNY MARKS
Music by JOHNNY MARKS

I'LL BE HOME FOR CHRISTMAS

Words and Music by KIM GANNON
and WALTER KENT

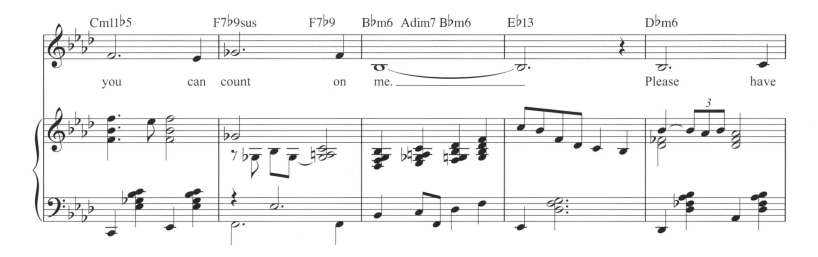

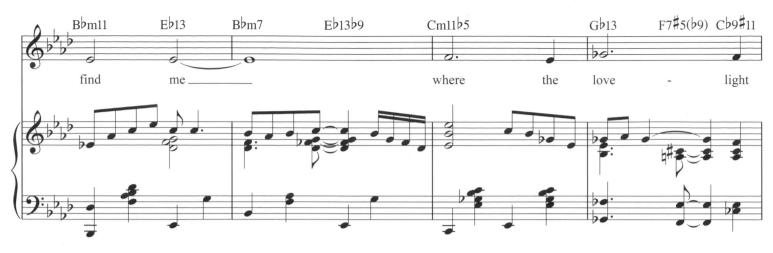

find me _____ where the love - light

gleams. _____ I'll be home for

Christ - mas, if on - ly in my

dreams. _____ dreams. _____

IT'S BEGINNING TO LOOK LIKE CHRISTMAS

By MEREDITH WILLSON

can - dy canes and sil - ver lanes a - glow.}
stur - dy kind that does - n't mind a snow.}
It's be -

gin - ning to look a lot like Christ - mas,
toys in ev - 'ry
soon the bells will

store.
start.
But the pret - ti - est sight to see is the
And the thing that will make them ring is the

hol - ly that will be on your own front'
car - ol that you sing right with - in your

To Coda $\oplus$

I'VE GOT MY LOVE TO KEEP ME WARM

from the 20th Century Fox Motion Picture ON THE AVENUE

Words and Music by
IRVING BERLIN

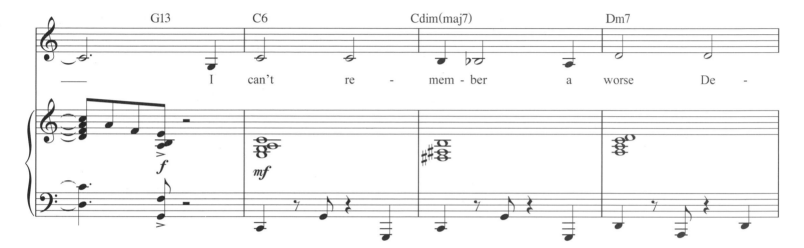

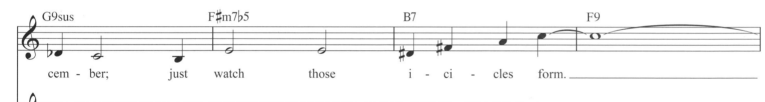

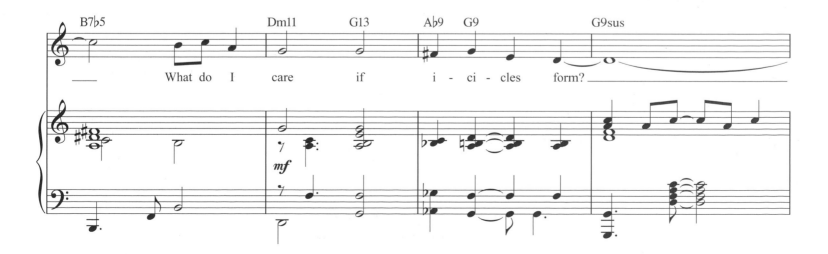

I've got my love to keep me warm.

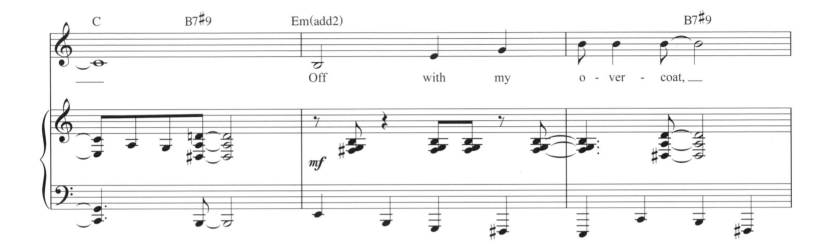

Off with my o-ver-coat, ___

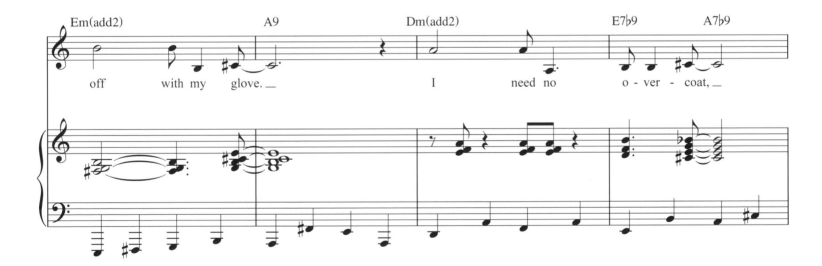

off with my glove. ___ I need no o-ver-coat, ___

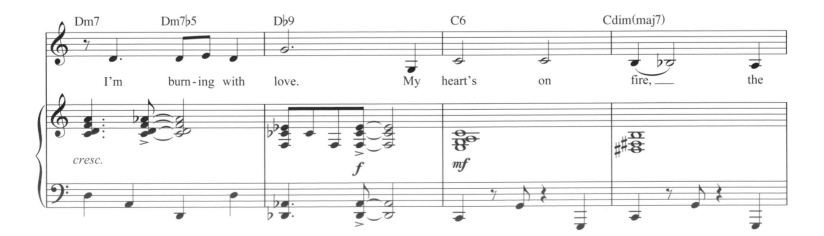

I'm burn-ing with love. My heart's on fire, ___ the

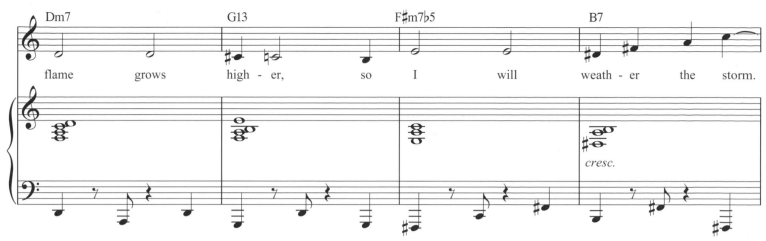

flame grows high-er, so I will weath-er the storm.

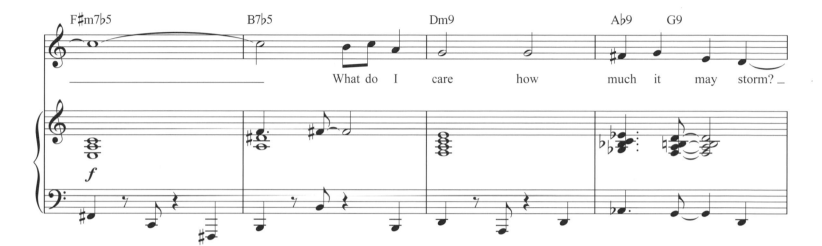

What do I care how much it may storm? _

I've got my love to keep me warm. _

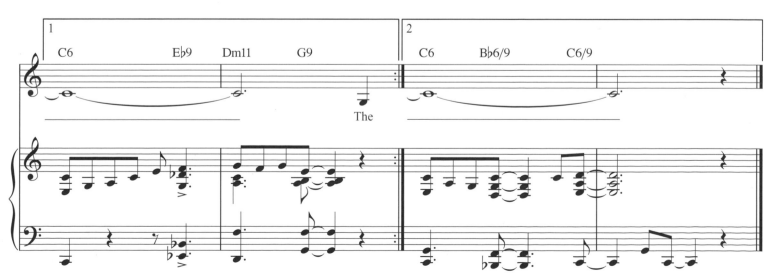

The

LET IT SNOW! LET IT SNOW! LET IT SNOW!

Words by SAMMY CAHN
Music by JULE STYNE

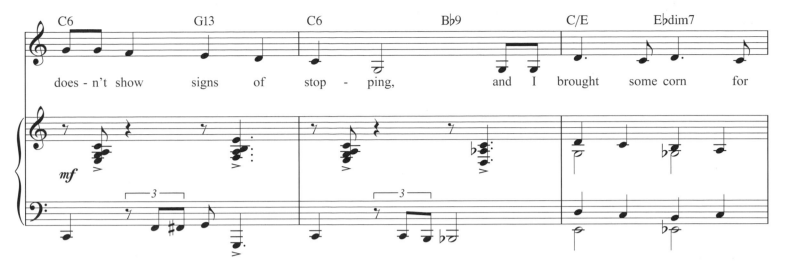

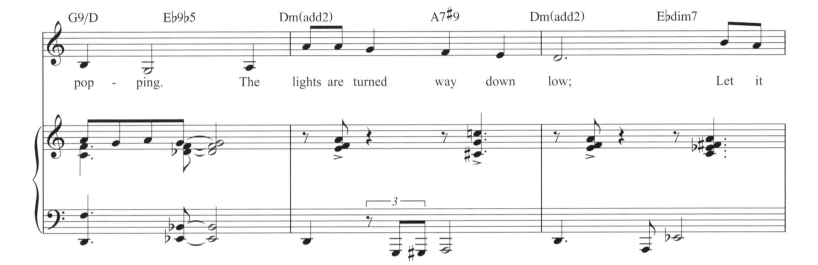

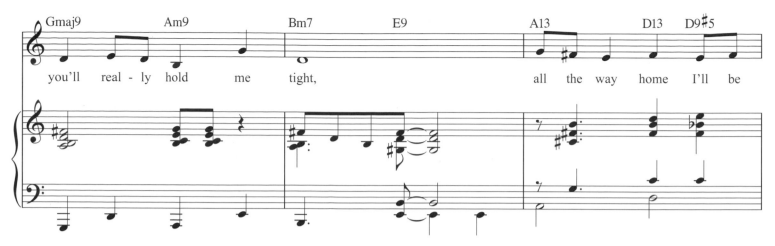

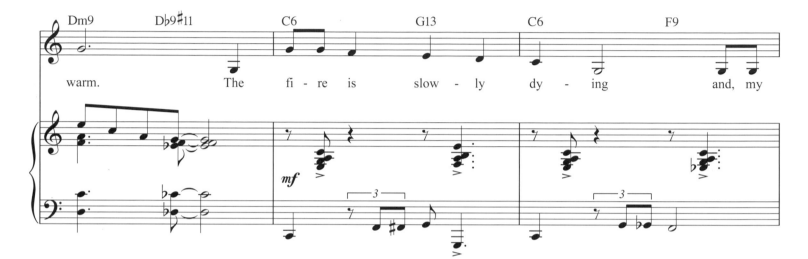

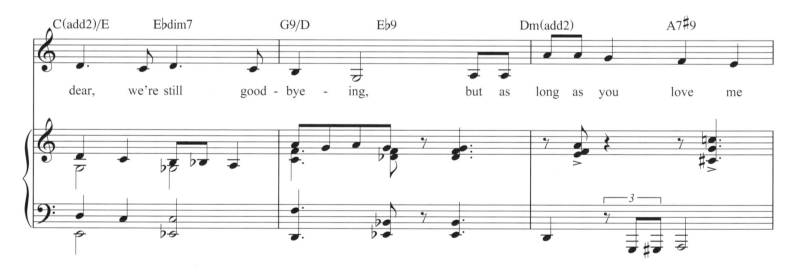

To Opt. Piano Solo

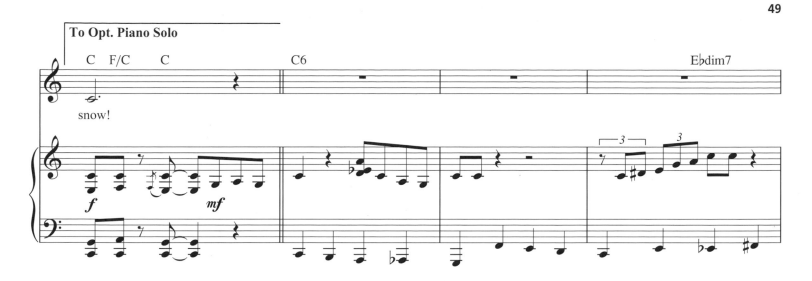

snow!

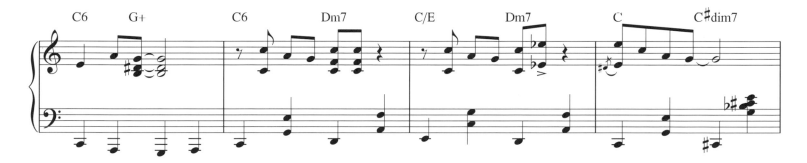

When we

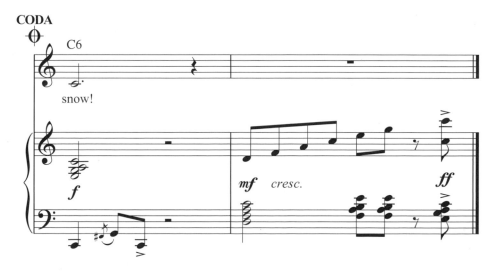

snow!

A MARSHMALLOW WORLD

Words by CARL SIGMAN
Music by PETER DE ROSE

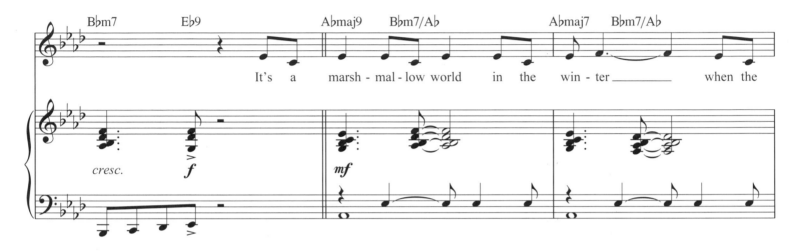

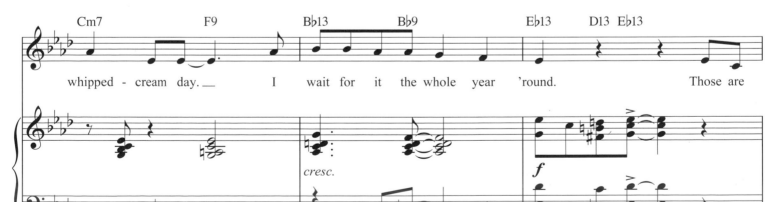

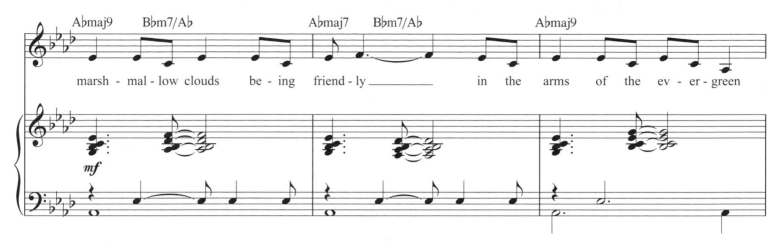

marsh-mal-low clouds be-ing friend-ly _____ in the arms of the ev-er-green

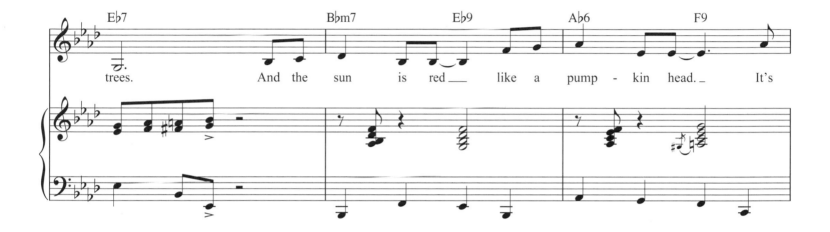

trees. And the sun is red __ like a pump-kin head. __ It's

shin-ing so your nose won't freeze. The world is your snow-ball,

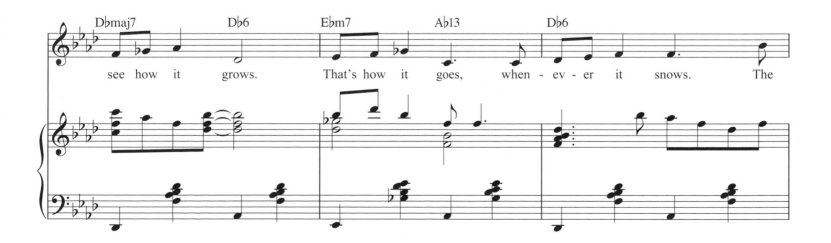

see how it grows. That's how it goes, when-ev-er it snows. The

world is your snow - ball, just for a song. Get out and roll it a -

long. It's a yum, yum - my world made for sweet - hearts. _____ Take a

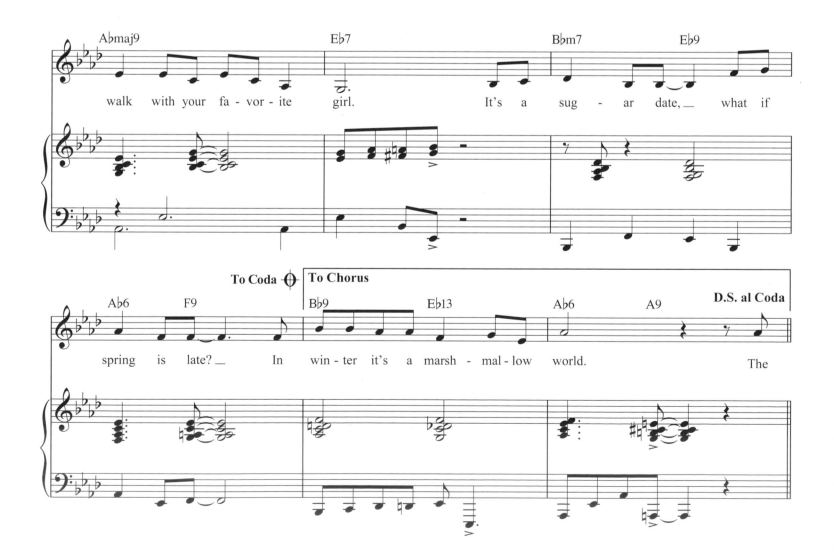

walk with your fa - vor - ite girl. It's a sug - ar date,_ what if

spring is late?_ In win - ter it's a marsh - mal - low world. The

To Coda ⊕   **To Chorus**   **D.S. al Coda**

To Opt. Piano Solo

win - ter it's a marsh - mal - low world.

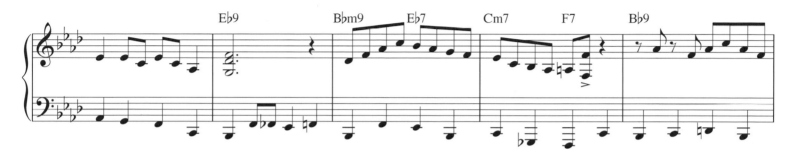

D.S. al Coda

The

CODA

win - ter it's a marsh - mal - low world.

ff

MARY, DID YOU KNOW?

Words and Music by MARK LOWRY
and BUDDY GREENE

Mar - y, did you know?

The blind will see, ___ the deaf will hear, ___ the

dead will live ___ a - gain, ___ the lame will leap, ___ the dumb will speak ___ the

prais - es of ___ the Lamb. ___ Mar - y, did you

D.S. al Coda

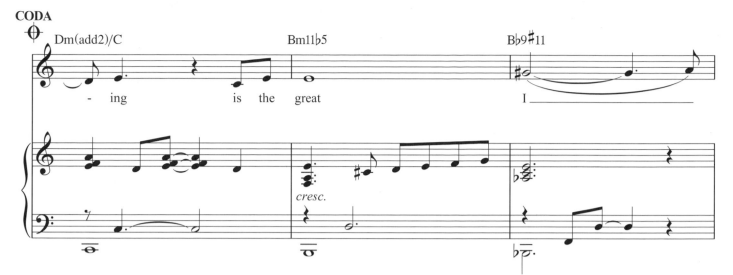

CODA

Dm(add2)/C   Bm11♭5   B♭9♯11

-ing   is the great   I _____

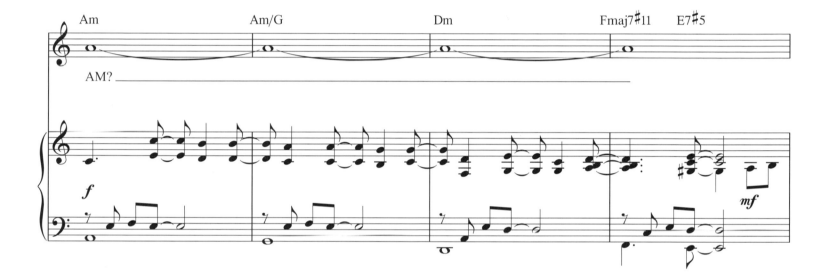

Am   Am/G   Dm   Fmaj7♯11   E7♯5

AM? _____

Am   Am/G

Fmaj7♯11   E7♯5   B♭9♯11   **Freely** Am(add2)   D13♯11

rit.

MERRY CHRISTMAS, DARLING

Words and Music by RICHARD CARPENTER
and FRANK POOLER

MISTLETOE AND HOLLY

Words and Music by FRANK SINATRA,
DOK STANFORD and HENRY W. SANICOLA

Slow Swing

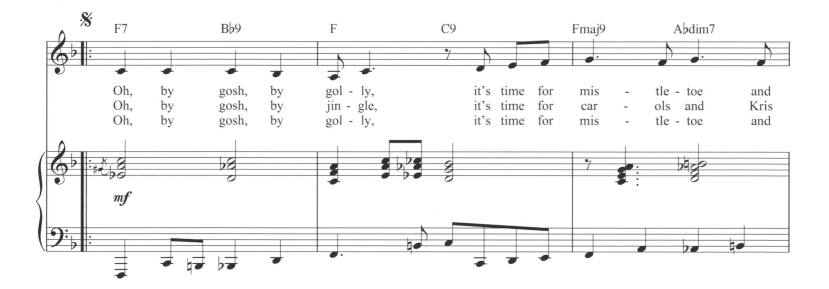

Oh, by gosh, by gol - ly, it's time for mis - tle - toe and
Oh, by gosh, by jin - gle, it's time for car - ols and Kris
Oh, by gosh, by gol - ly, it's time for mis - tle - toe and

To Coda ⊕

hol - ly, tast - y pheas - ants, Christ - mas pres - ents,
Krin - gle, o - ver - eat - ing, mer - ry greet - ings
hol - ly, fan - cy ties an' gran - ny's pies an'

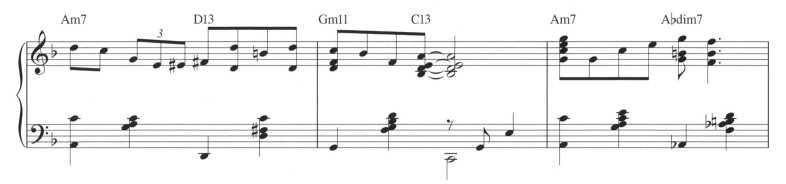

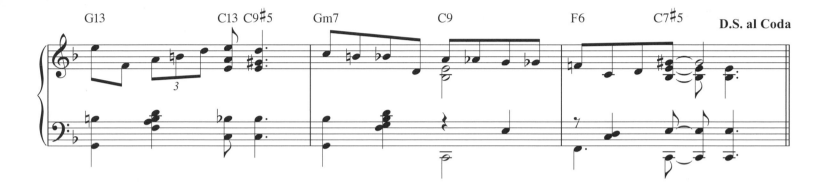

D.S. al Coda

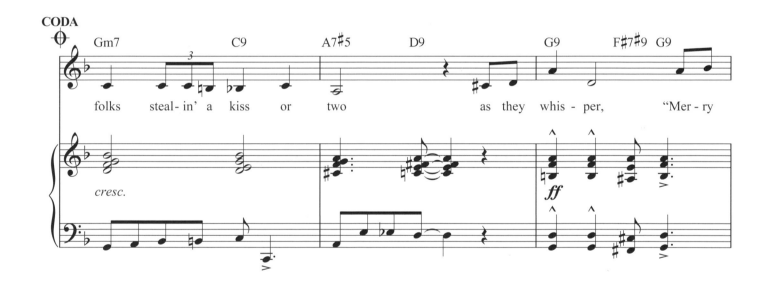

folks steal- in' a kiss or two as they whis - per, "Mer - ry

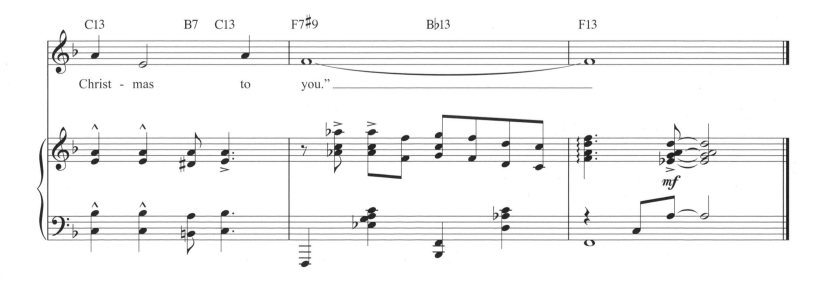

Christ - mas to you." _____

THE MOST WONDERFUL TIME OF THE YEAR

Words and Music by EDDIE POLA
and GEORGE WYLE

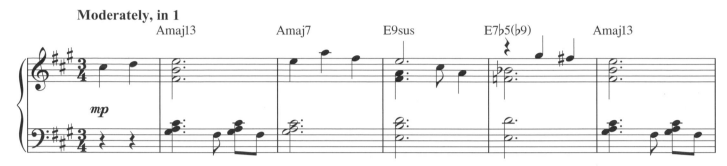

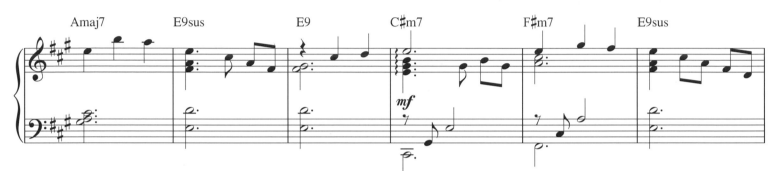

It's the

most won-der-ful time _____ of the year, _____
hap - hap-pi-est sea - son of all, _____
most won-der-ful time _____ of the year.

CODA

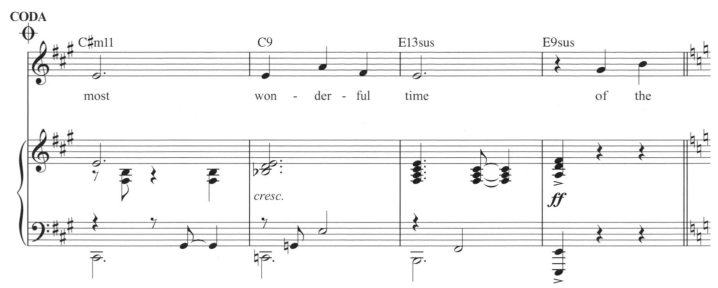

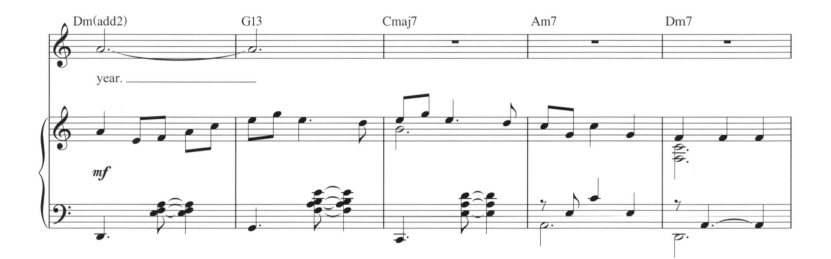

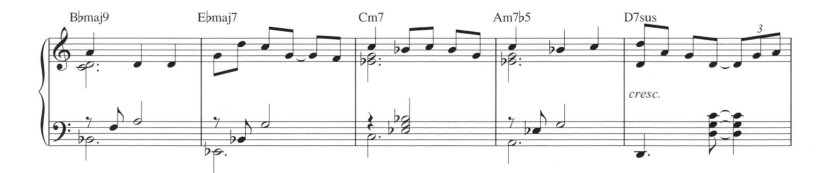

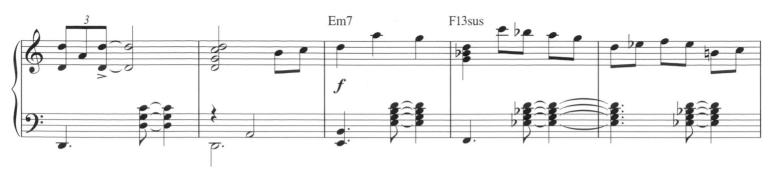

It's the most won-der-ful time of the

year._____ There'll be much mis-tle-toe-ing and

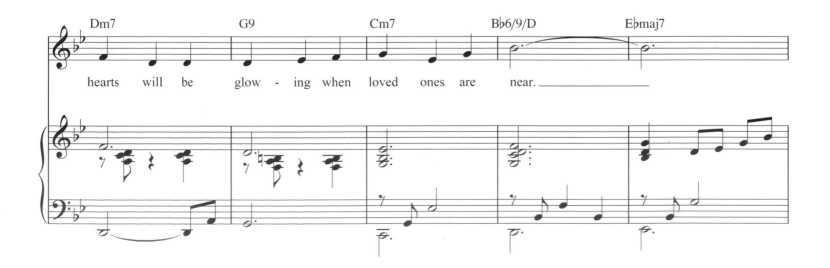

hearts will be glow-ing when loved ones are near._____

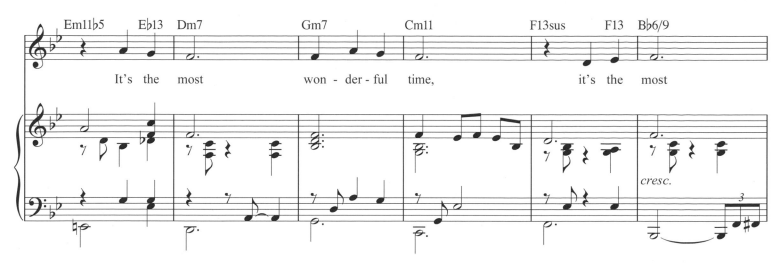

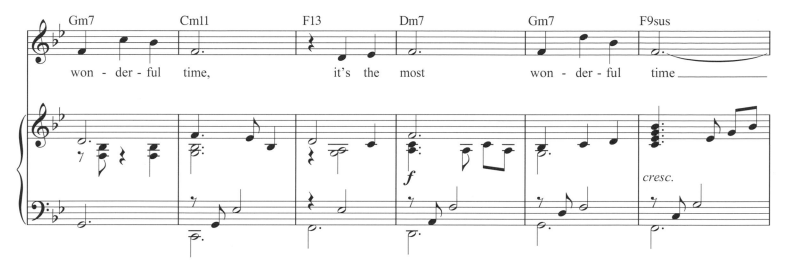

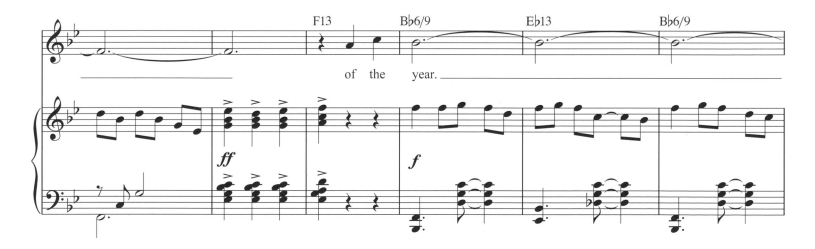

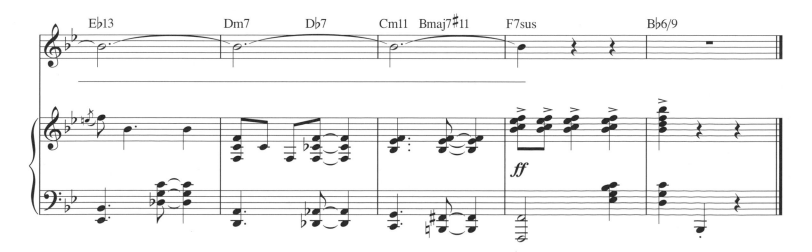

ROCKIN' AROUND THE CHRISTMAS TREE

Music and Lyrics by
JOHNNY MARKS

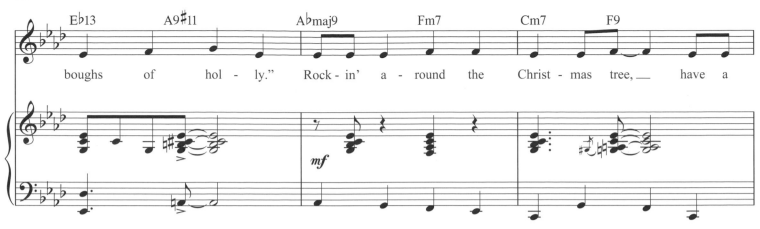

boughs of hol - ly." Rock - in' a - round the Christ - mas tree, __ have a

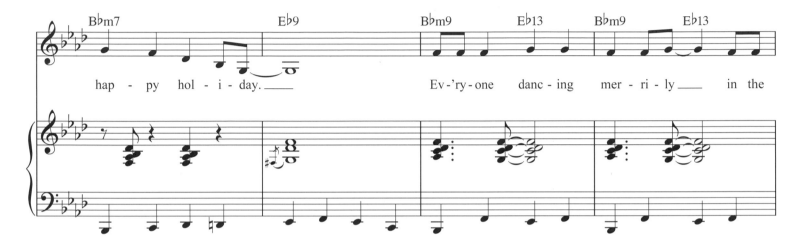

hap - py hol - i - day.____ Ev - 'ry - one danc - ing mer - ri - ly___ in the

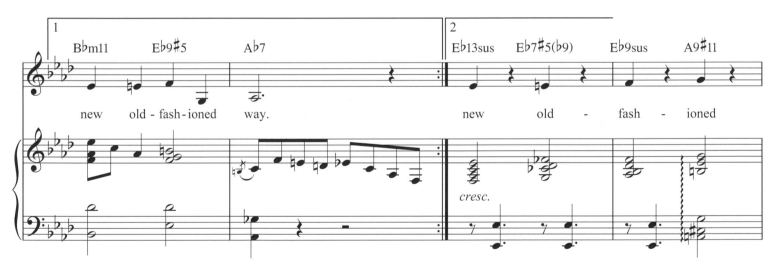

new old - fash - ioned way.   new old - fash - ioned

way. _____

RUDOLPH THE RED-NOSED REINDEER

Music and Lyrics by
JOHNNY MARKS

Moderately fast, lightly

Freely

You know Dash-er and Danc-er and Pranc-er and Vix-en,

Com-et and Cu-pid and Don-ner and Blitz-en, but do you re-

call the most fa-mous rein-deer of all?

Light Latin feel

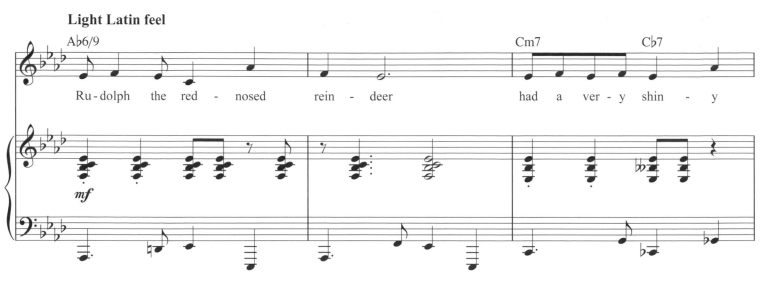

Ru - dolph the red - nosed rein - deer had a ver - y shin - y

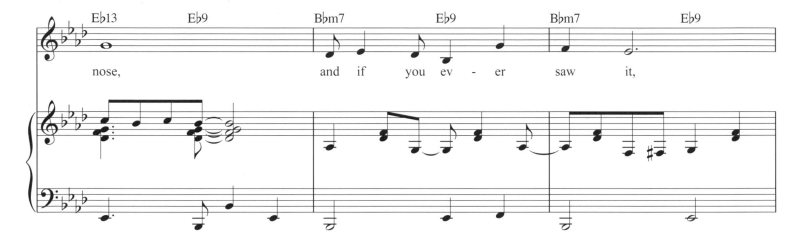

nose, and if you ev - er saw it,

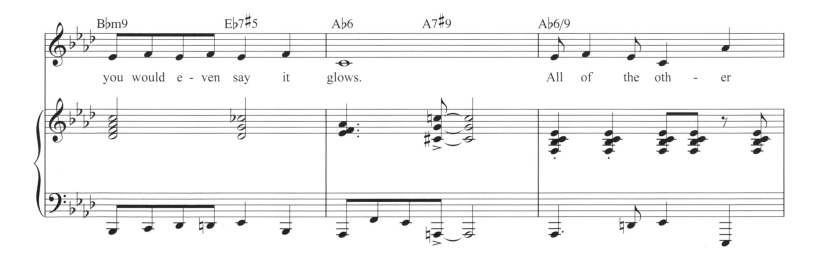

you would e - ven say it glows. All of the oth - er

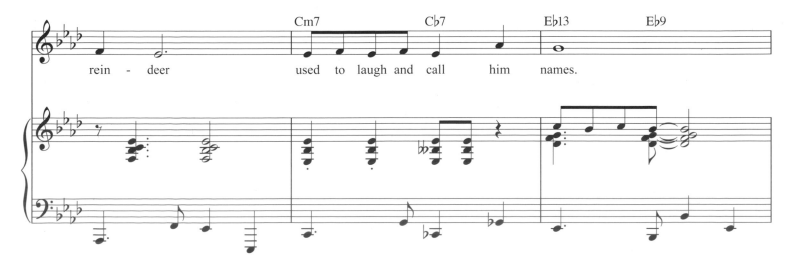

rein - deer used to laugh and call him names.

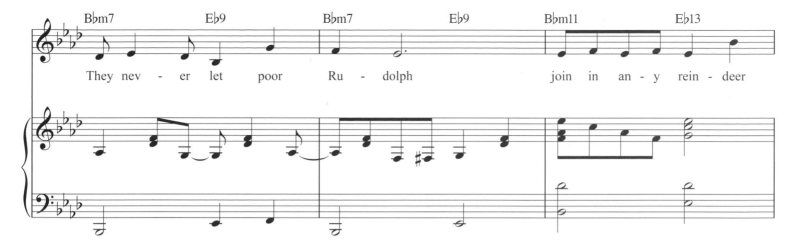

They nev - er let poor Ru - dolph join in an - y rein - deer

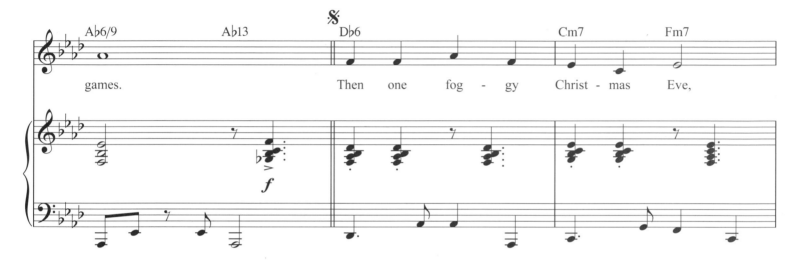

games. Then one fog - gy Christ - mas Eve,

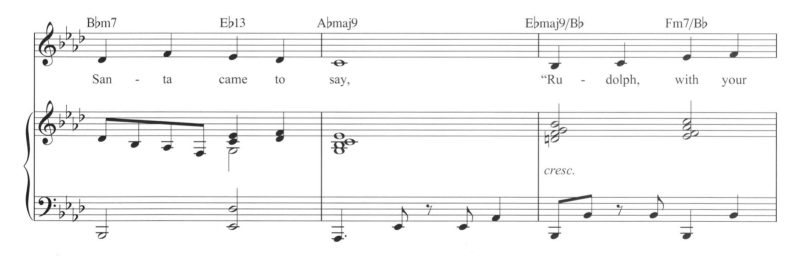

San - ta came to say, "Ru - dolph, with your

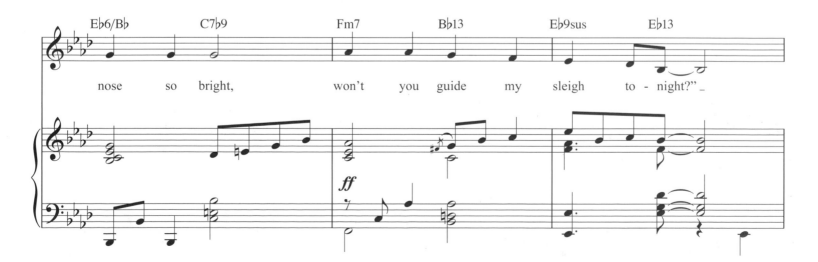

nose so bright, won't you guide my sleigh to - night?"

Then how the rein - deer loved him, as they shout-ed out with

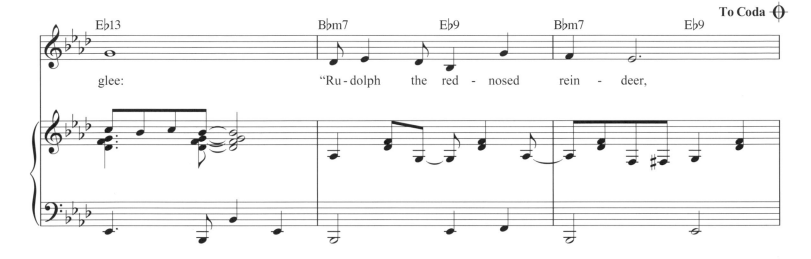

glee: "Ru - dolph the red - nosed rein - deer,

To Chorus   **D.S. al Coda**   **To Opt. Piano Solo**

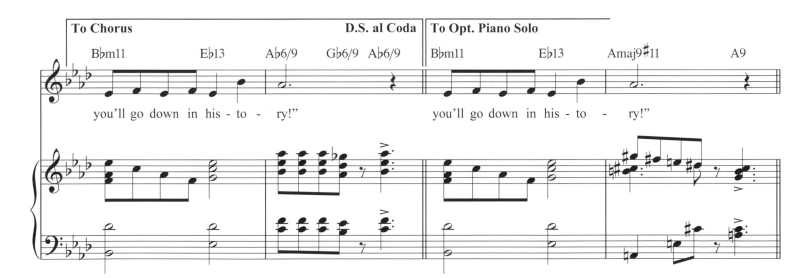

you'll go down in his - to - ry!"   you'll go down in his - to - ry!"

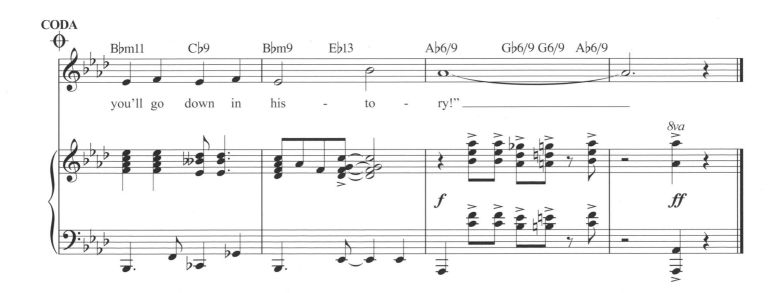

you'll go down in his - to - ry!"

SANTA BABY

By JOAN JAVITS,
PHIL SPRINGER and TONY SPRINGER

Freely, with a Bluesy feel

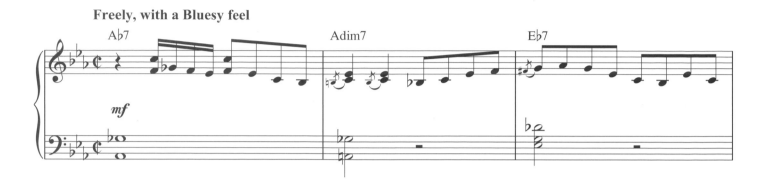

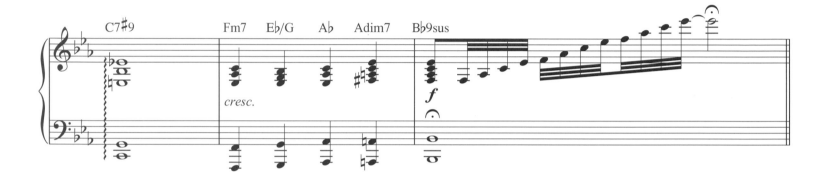

Moderately slow Swing

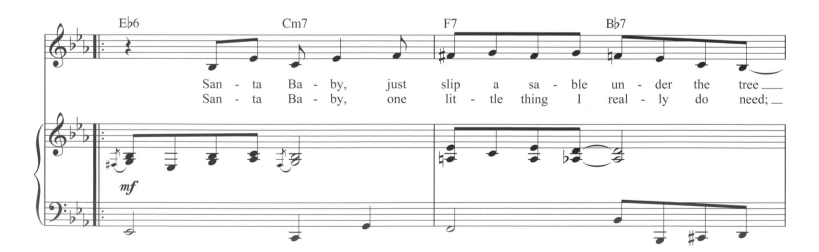

San - ta Ba - by, just slip a sa - ble un - der the tree ___
San - ta Ba - by, one lit - tle thing I real - ly do need; ___

for me. ____ Been an aw-ful good girl, ____ San-ta Ba-by, so
the deed ____ to a plat-i-num mine, ____ San-ta hon-ey, so

hur-ry down the chim-ney to - night. ____
hur-ry down the chim-ney to - night. ____

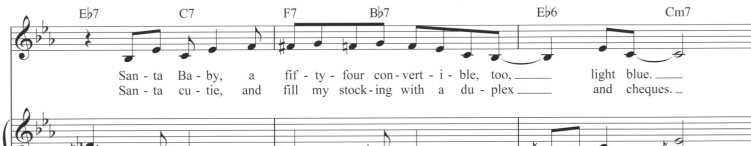

San - ta Ba-by, a fif-ty - four con-vert-i - ble, too, ____ light blue. ____
San - ta cu-tie, and fill my stock-ing with a du-plex ____ and cheques. ____

I'll wait up for you, dear ____ San-ta Ba-by, so hur-ry down the chim-ney to - night. ____
Sign your X on the line, ____ San-ta cu-tie, and hur-ry down the chim-ney to - night. ____

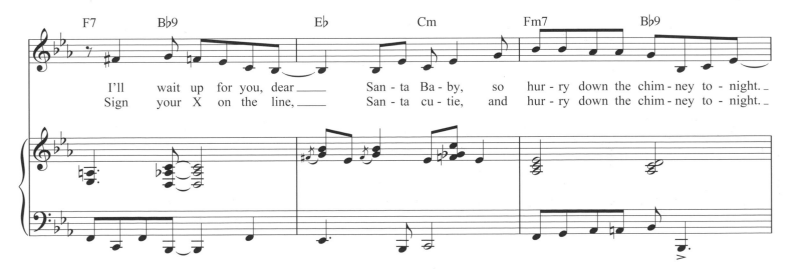

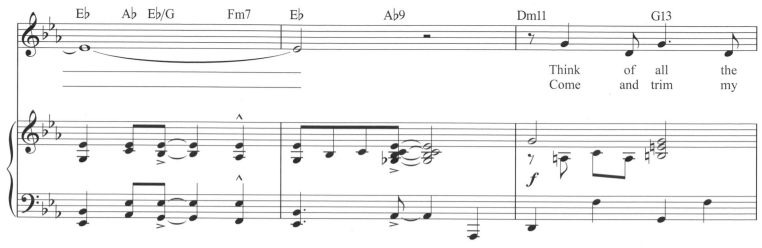

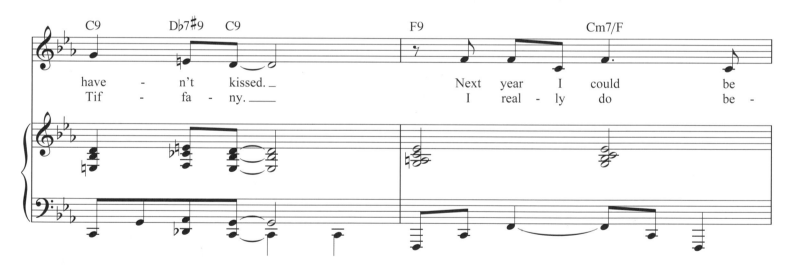

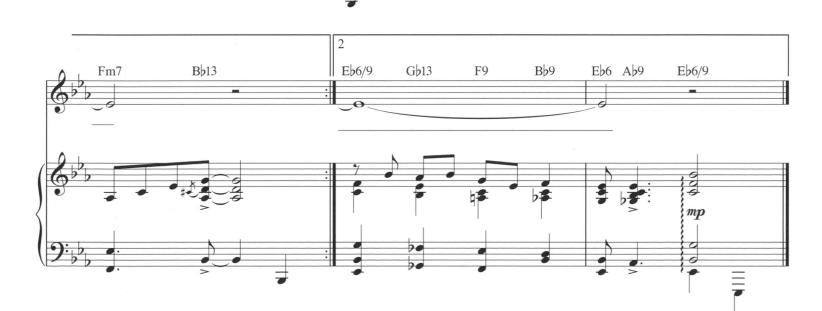

SANTA CLAUS IS COMIN' TO TOWN

Words by HAVEN GILLESPIE
Music by J. FRED COOTS

make-ing a list and check-ing it twice, gon-na find out who's naugh-ty and nice.

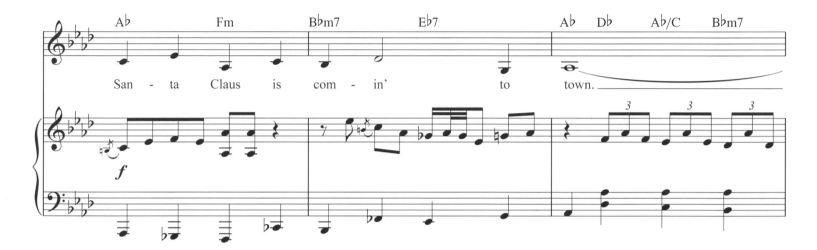

San - ta Claus is com - in' to town. _____

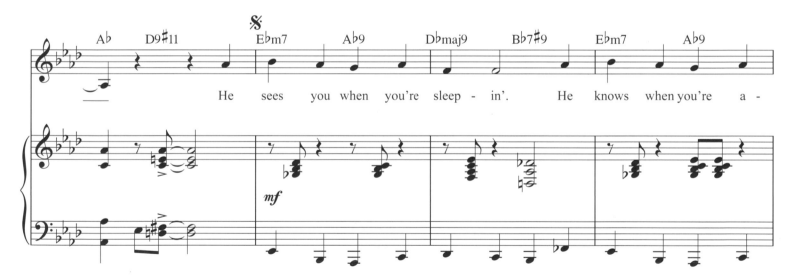

He sees you when you're sleep - in'. He knows when you're a -

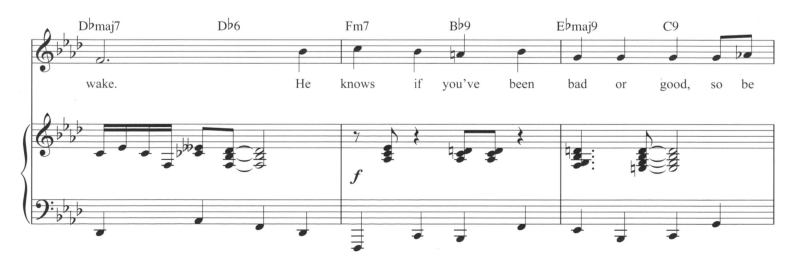

wake. He knows if you've been bad or good, so be

good for good- ness' sake. Oh! You bet- ter watch out, you bet- ter not cry,

To Coda

bet- ter not pout, I'm tell- ing you why: San- ta Claus is

To Chorus **D.S. al Coda**

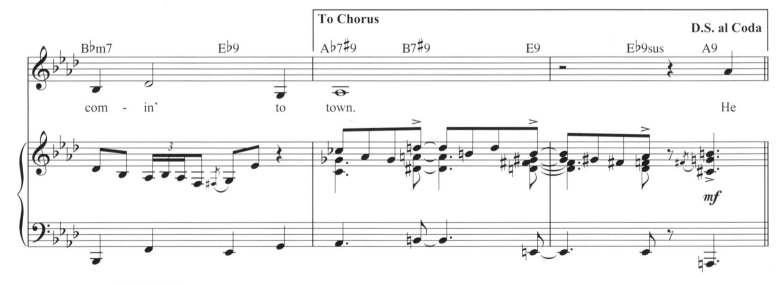

com- in' to town. He

To Opt. Piano Solo

town.

D.S. al Coda

He

CODA

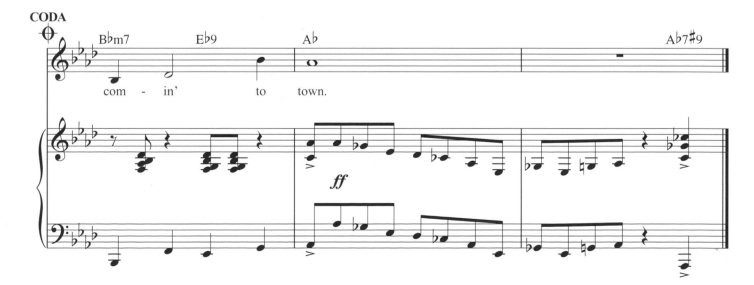

com - in'   to   town.

SILVER BELLS

from the Paramount Picture THE LEMON DROP KID

Words and Music by JAY LIVINGSTON
and RAY EVANS

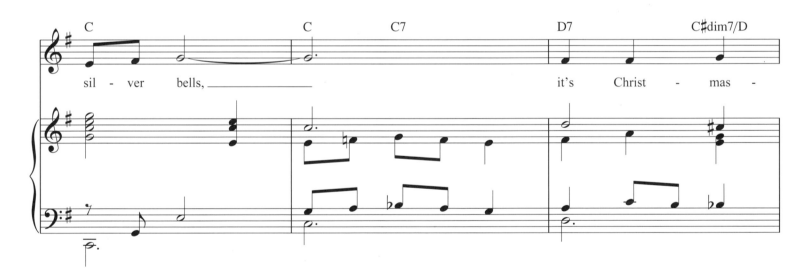

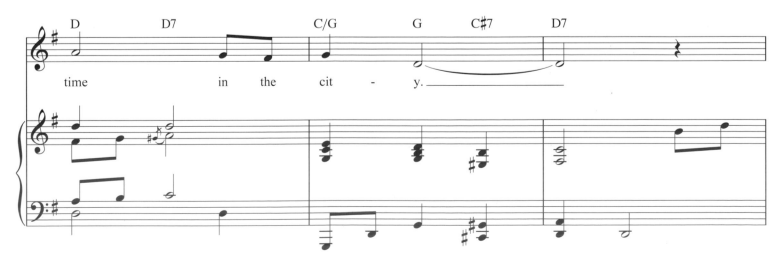

SLEIGH RIDE

Music by LEROY ANDERSON
Words by MITCHELL PARISH

Moderately bright Swing

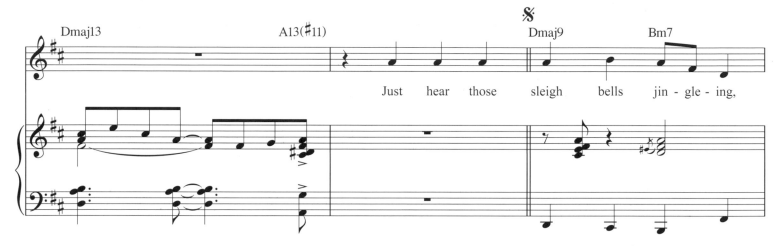

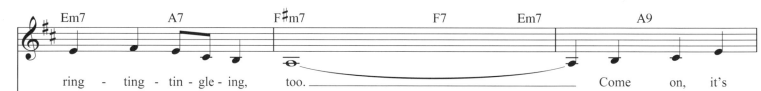

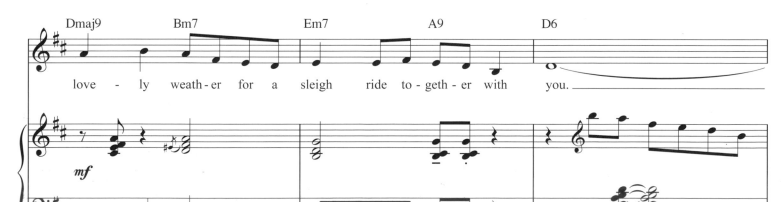

Just hear those sleigh bells jin-gle-ing, ring-ting-tin-gle-ing, too. _____ Come on, it's love-ly weath-er for a sleigh ride to-geth-er with you. _____

Out - side the snow is fall - ing and friends are call - ing, "Yoo

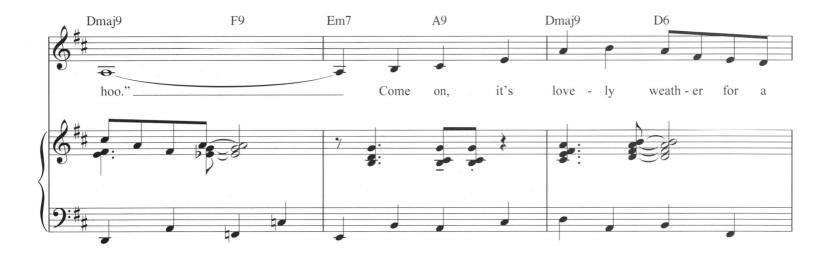

hoo." _____ Come on, it's love - ly weath - er for a

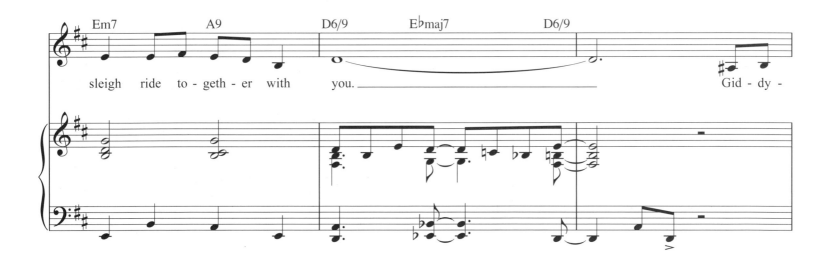

sleigh ride to - geth - er with you. _____ Gid - dy -

yap, gid - dy - yap, gid - dy - yap, let's go, let's look at the

We're rid-ing in a won-der-land of snow. _____ Gid-dy - yap, gid-dy-yap, gid-dy-

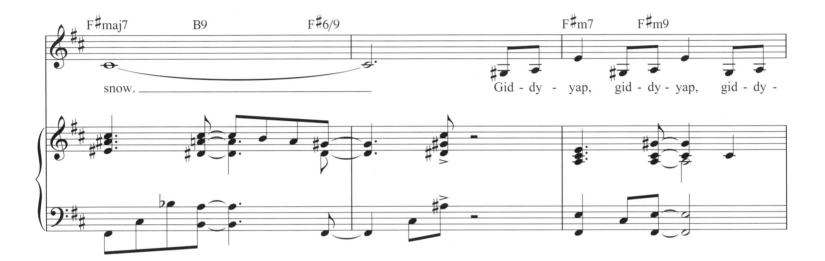

yap, it's grand, just hold-ing your hand.

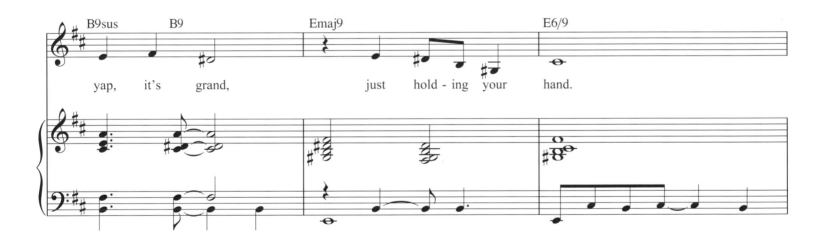

We're glid-ing a - long with a song of a win-ter - y fair-y-

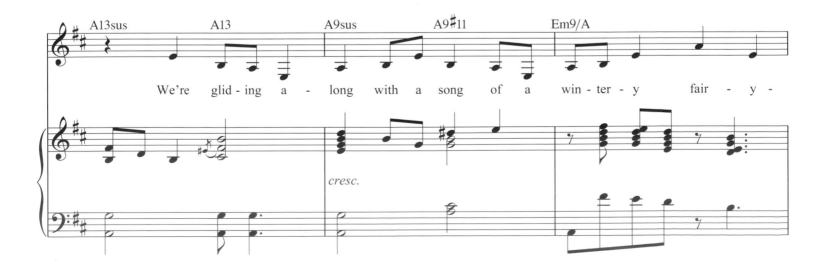

cresc.

WHITE CHRISTMAS
from the Motion Picture Irving Berlin's HOLIDAY INN

Words and Music by
IRVING BERLIN

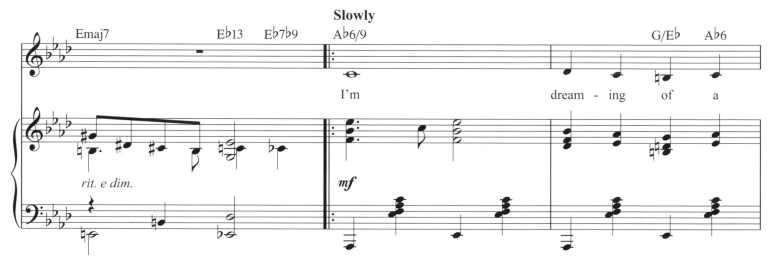

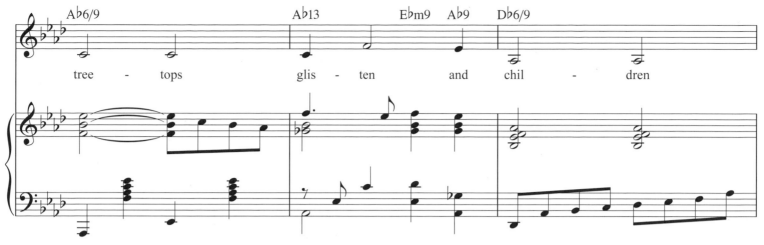

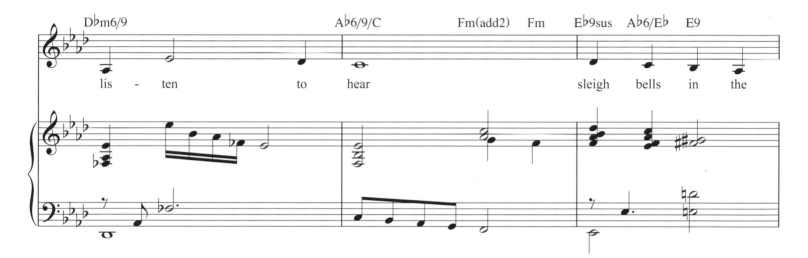

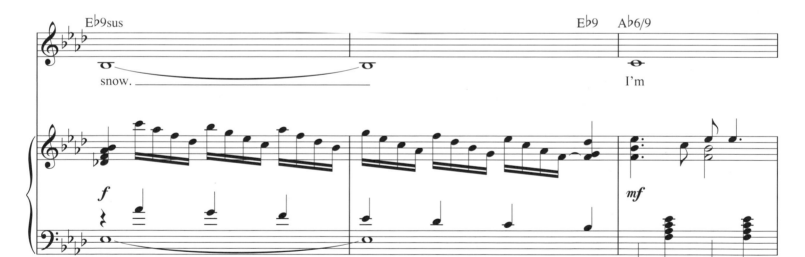

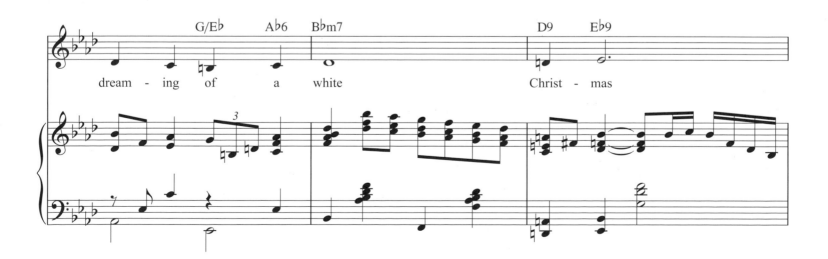

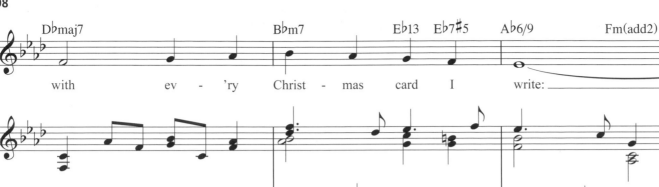

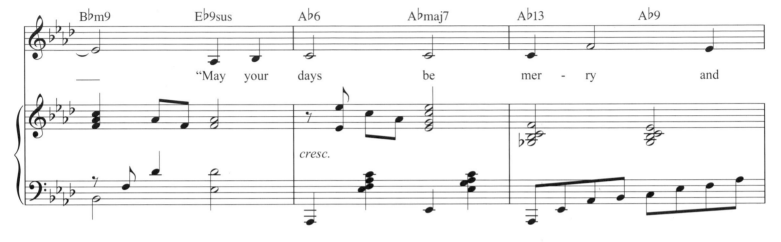

with ev - 'ry Christ - mas card I write: _____

"May your days be mer - ry and

bright _____ and may all your Christ - mas - es be

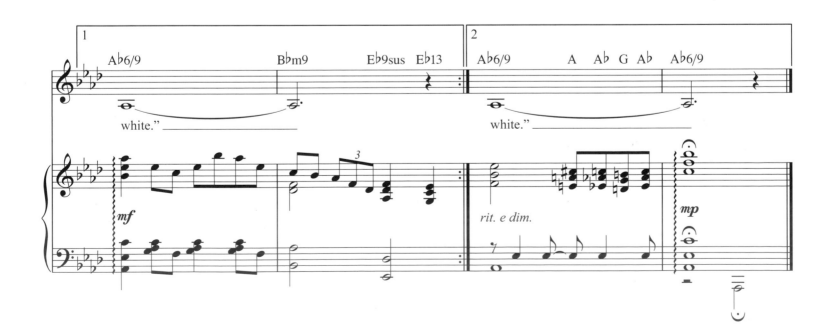

white." _____

white."

WINTER WONDERLAND

Words by DICK SMITH
Music by FELIX BERNARD

Moderate Swing

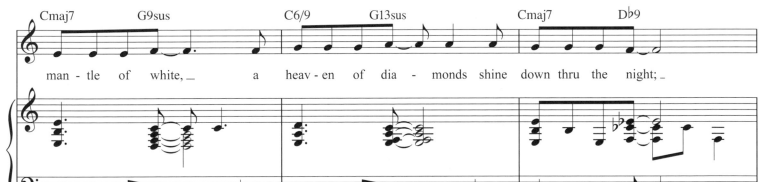

Love knows no sea - son; love knows no clime; _

ro - mance can blos - som an - y old time. _ Here in the o - pen, we're

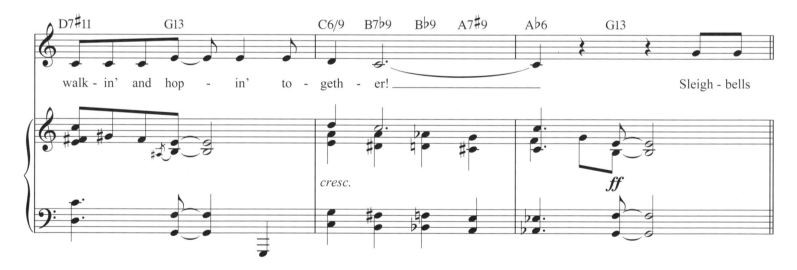

walk - in' and hop - in' to - geth - er! _____ Sleigh - bells

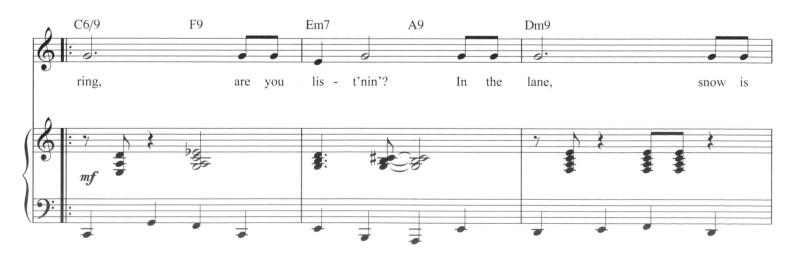

ring, are you lis - t'nin'? In the lane, snow is

ORIGINAL KEYS FOR SINGERS

Titles in the Original Keys for Singers series are designed for vocalists looking for authentic transcriptions from their favorite artists. The books transcribe famous vocal performances exactly as recorded and provide piano accompaniment parts so that you can perform or pratice exactly as Ella or Patsy or Josh!

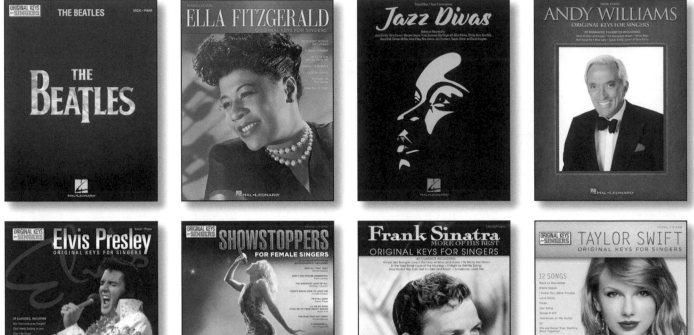

ACROSS THE UNIVERSE
00307010...$19.95

ADELE
00155395...$19.99

LOUIS ARMSTRONG
00307029...$19.99

THE BEATLES
00307400...$19.99

BROADWAY HITS (FEMALE SINGERS)
00119085...$19.99

BROADWAY HITS (MALE SINGERS)
00119084...$19.99

PATSY CLINE
00740072...$22.99

ELLA FITZGERALD
00740252...$22.99

JOSH GROBAN
00306969...$19.99

BILLIE HOLIDAY
Transcribed from Historic Recordings
00740140...$19.99

ETTA JAMES: GREATEST HITS
00130427...$19.99

JAZZ DIVAS
00114959...$19.99

LADIES OF CHRISTMAS
00312192...$19.99

NANCY LAMOTT
00306995...$19.99

MEN OF CHRISTMAS
00312241...$19.99

THE BETTE MIDLER SONGBOOK
00307067...$19.99

THE BEST OF LIZA MINNELLI
00306928...$19.99

ONCE
00102569...$16.99

ELVIS PRESLEY
00138200...$19.99

SHOWSTOPPERS FOR FEMALE SINGERS
00119640...$19.99

BEST OF NINA SIMONE
00121576...$19.99

FRANK SINATRA – MORE OF HIS BEST
00307081...$19.99

TAYLOR SWIFT
00142702...$16.99

SARAH VAUGHAN
00306558...$24.99

VOCAL POP
00312656...$19.99

ANDY WILLIAMS – CHRISTMAS COLLECTION
00307158...$17.99

ANDY WILLIAMS
00307160...$17.99

HAL•LEONARD®
www.halleonard.com

Prices, contents, and availability subject to change without notice.